The Pilgrim's Progress, Part 2
Study Guide

Christiana's Journey

A Bible Study Based on John Bunyan's
The Pilgrim's Progress, Part 2

By Alan Vermilye

The Pilgrim's Progress, Part 2 Study Guide:
A Bible Study Based on John Bunyan's The Pilgrim's Progress, Part 2

Copyright © 2023 Alan Vermilye
Brown Chair Books

To learn more about this Bible study, to order additional copies, or to download the answer guide, visit **www.BrownChairBooks.com**.

Version 1

Table of Contents

Required Book for Study

Do you have the right book for this study?

Although there are many versions of this Bunyan classic, *The Pilgrim's Progress, Part 2, Christiana's Journey: A Readable Modern-Day Version of The Pilgrim's Progress, Part 2* is the only book that is made specifically for this study.

The study guide's questions are written to be used alongside each chapter in the book. Other "readable" versions will feel drastically different and will not match up with the study questions and format of this study. In addition, many leave out key text and do not keep with Bunyan's original intentions for the book.

If you are completing this study in a group setting, it would also be helpful if each participant had the same book to make class discussion time more beneficial.

Learn more about this book at www.BrownChairBooks.com.

Course Notes and Study Format

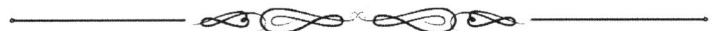

The Pilgrim's Progress, Part 2 Study Guide contains six weekly study sessions corresponding with the thirty chapters of *The Pilgrim's Progress, Part 2, Christiana's Journey: A Readable Modern-Day Version of The Pilgrim's Progress, Part 2.* This study guide is for individual study or for weekly small groups that gather to discuss each chapter.

HOW TO USE THIS STUDY GUIDE

There are five chapters for each weekly session, with three questions for each chapter, allowing for plenty of time to read each chapter and answer questions in one week's time.

As you read, make notes in your book, and underline or highlight sections that interest you. As you work through each session, make a note of other questions or observations that you would like to share in your small group time.

Session 1	Chapters 1–5 (plus Introduction)
Session 2	Chapters 6–10
Session 3	Chapters 11–15
Session 4	Chapters 16–20
Session 5	Chapters 21–25
Session 6	Chapters 26–30

SMALL GROUP FORMAT

The study is ideal for Sunday school classes and midweek times at the church or in the homes of small group members. Session length is variable, but ideally, allow at least 60–90 minutes per session. You will most likely not be able to get through all the questions in a single session, so pick the questions you want to make sure you cover.

Pace yourself or your group, and do not rush the study. If you feel you need additional weeks for certain sections, be flexible, and allow the learning process and class discussion to happen naturally. It's most helpful for learning if each person has their own book and study guide and works through the questions prior to each class. However, couples might find it convenient to share a book.

ANSWER AND SCRIPTURE REFERENCE GUIDES

The answers to each question and a Scripture Reference Guide are available for free at www.BrownChairBooks.com. However, do not cheat yourself. Work through each session prior to viewing the answers. The Scripture Reference Guide is a handy tool that saves valuable class time in looking up Bible passages.

Author Summary

John Bunyan was born in Elstow, near Bedford, England, in 1628. His parents were poor, and his father was a metalworker, or "tinker," who traveled around mending pots and pans; John followed in his father's trade. He had no formal education but learned to read and write.

Although we have few details about his early life, in his autobiography, *Grace Abounding to the Chief of Sinners*, he tells us his parents did not encourage him in matters of spirituality at home. He was rough, enjoyed dancing and playing tipcat, and was given to "cursing, swearing, lying, and blaspheming the holy name of God."

In 1644 Bunyan lost both his mother and sister Margaret. Later that same year, when an edict demanded 225 recruits from Bedford, he entered the Parliamentary Army as a private at sixteen.

There are few details about his military service, which took place during the English Civil War. However, during one battle, a fellow soldier died when he requested to go forward in Bunyan's place. This dramatic event led Bunyan to believe God had spared his life for some purpose. His military service exposed him to a variety of religious sects while indulging in all sorts of ungodly behavior.

Bunyan spent nearly three years in the army before returning home in 1647 to continue his trade as a metalworker. His father was now remarried and had more children, so Bunyan moved to a cottage in Elstow High Street.

His first marriage, in 1648, was to a girl who was poor like himself but came from a godly family. Her name is unknown, but she owned two books, of which Bunyan said, "Her only portion was two volumes which her father had given her, 'The Plain Man's Pathway' and 'The Practice of Piety.' In these I sometimes read, wherein I found some things pleasant to me."

During his first five years of marriage, his wife would have a profound influence on his life as he attended church regularly and gave up his sinful life. He also pored over the Scriptures, leading him to his own thoughts about the conviction that he would later write about in detail.

He joined a Baptist society at Bedford and by 1653 had become a lay preacher as a member of the congregation at Bedford. Over time, Bunyan's popularity exploded, and great crowds in the thousands would come to hear him preach.

Their first child, Mary, was born blind in 1650. They would have three more children: Elizabeth, Thomas, and John. But in 1658, ten years into their marriage, Bunyan's wife died, leaving him with four small children under ten. A year later, in 1659, he got remarried to an eighteen-year-old young woman named Elizabeth.

However, their first year of marriage was interrupted when the religious tolerance that had allowed Bunyan to preach was curtailed when the monarchy was restored to power. In 1660 King Charles II came to the throne and ordered that all preachers that did not belong to the Church of England be imprisoned or banished.

Bunyan could no longer preach at the Anglican church where his congregation met. Still, he continued preaching in other places and later that year was warned that he would soon be arrested. He refused to escape and was arrested and sentenced to three months' imprisonment. They threatened him with more jail time, banishment from England, and possible execution if he did not agree to stop preaching.

Although he could have his freedom whenever he wanted it, Bunyan refused to renounce preaching, opting to stand firm and keep a clear conscience instead; he was imprisoned for a total of twelve years in the Bedford County Jail.

Bunyan's imprisonment brought great hardship to his family. Elizabeth, who was pregnant at the time of his arrest, would later give birth to a stillborn child. She continually attempted to secure her husband's release while caring for Bunyan's four small children, one of whom was blind. She relied on the charity of fellow church members and on what little Bunyan could earn in prison making shoelaces.

Occasionally they allowed him out of prison, where he attended the Bedford meetings and even preached. His daughter Sarah was born during his imprisonment, and a son, Joseph, was born after his release.

While imprisoned, he became the pastor of a congregation of inmates and stayed busy writing religious tracts, sermons, and nine books, including *Grace Abounding to the Chief of Sinners*, which was published in 1666. In 1671 King Charles II issued a declaration of religious indulgences that released thousands of non-conformists from prison, including Bunyan, in 1672.

He immediately returned to preaching but three years later was imprisoned again for around six months. It was during this time that he began work on *The Pilgrim's Progress*, which was published after his release.

Bunyan was never jailed again but spent the last fifteen years of his life preaching all over England, including a visit to London every year to deliver sermons to large Baptist congregations.

In August 1688, on his way to London to preach, Bunyan went to Reading Berkshire on a ministerial visit to help resolve a quarrel between a father and a son. As he returned to London on horseback, he got caught in a heavy rainstorm and fell ill with a violent fever, dying at the age of sixty.

He died at the house of his friend, John Strudwick, a grocer and chandler on Snow Hill in Holborn. His grave lies in the cemetery at Bunhill Fields in London.

Book Summary

John Bunyan completed the first part of *The Pilgrim's Progress*, featuring the journey of Christian, in 1678. After much demand for the sequel, Bunyan published *The Pilgrim's Progress, Part 2* in 1684, featuring the journey of Christian's wife, Christiana, and their four children.

As in the first story, the sequel is told from the narrator's perspective, as if he were in a dream. In this dream, the narrator tells the story of Christian's wife and children, whom he left behind in the City of Destruction after beginning his own pilgrimage to the Celestial City. Though his family were once rude and hostile to Christian's declaration of faith, they are now awakened to the realities of sin and judgment in their own lives.

The story begins with the narrator encountering a wise man named Mr. Sagacity, who informs him that Christian's wife, Christiana, and their four boys have begun their own pilgrimage to the Celestial City. He tells of Christiana's grief after losing her husband and recalls her vivid memories of his suffering and agony. Now filled with guilt for dismissing him as insane, she, too, battles those same feelings that Christian did, under the weight and burden of her own sin.

The next morning, after a fretful night of dreaming about the heavenly country, a man named Secret comes knocking at Christiana's door. This heavenly visitor provides an official invitation from the King to leave the City of Destruction and come to the Celestial City.

As Christiana and the boys are preparing to leave on their journey, some neighboring women named Mrs. Nervousness and Mercy come to visit. The elder, Mrs. Nervousness, tries to talk Christiana out of such a rash decision, citing all the danger that lies ahead, not to mention how reckless it would be to bring the children. Christiana refuses to listen to the older woman and asks them to leave. Intrigued by Christiana's claims, Mercy joins the family on their journey, all to the disdain of Mrs. Nervousness.

No sooner have they set out than they arrive at the Swamp of Despair, where they manage the swamp with little difficulty. It's at this point in the dream where Mr. Sagacity leaves and the narrator continues the rest of the story as if watching it unfold.

When the women and children arrive at the Wicket Gate, the Gate Keeper admits Christiana and boys but leaves Mercy outside the gate. As Christiana intercedes for her friend, Mercy is so overcome with fear that she faints. Eventually the Gate Keeper admits Mercy and sets them on their journey to the Celestial City on a path referred to as the Way.

No sooner have they entered the Way than the boys ignore their mother's warning and eat fruit that is hanging over the wall from the devil's orchard. Shortly thereafter, they encounter two wicked men on the path, who attack Christiana and Mercy. As the women cry for help, a Reliever comes to their rescue as the men escape over the wall. The Reliever is curious why they didn't ask the Lord for a guide while at the gate. It was then Christiana realizes the significance of the warnings from her dreams prior to leaving home and blames herself for their troubles.

Next, they arrive at the Interpreter's House, where they are shown all the same rooms shown to Christian. They are also shown new rooms to help them better understand their faith. Before leaving, they are cleaned and dressed for their journey and sent on their way with a brave guide named Great Heart.

When they arrive at the cross and tomb, Great Heart expounds upon the righteousness of Jesus Christ. He explains how Christ's obedience to God in suffering for the sins of man provides righteousness for others.

The guide then leads the group up the Hill of Difficulty, arriving at the same shady arbor where Christian fell asleep and lost his scroll. Like her husband, Christiana leaves her bottle of spirits behind in the arbor and has to send one of her sons back to retrieve it.

Then they come to where Mistrust and Nervousness met Christian to persuade him to turn back for fear of the lions. Now a stage is there, marking the place where the two men were burned with a hot iron for interfering with Christian's journey.

After passing this site, they encounter the lions and a giant named Grim, who tries to prevent the pilgrims from passing. Great Heart defeats the giant, and they pass by the lions without incident.

Great Heart successfully guides the pilgrims to the Palace Beautiful, where Watchful and a group of four sisters admit them into the palace. After agreeing to stay for a month, one sister, Prudence, asks Christiana for permission to examine the boy's' understanding of their faith. As she questions each boy, they impress her with their knowledge of Scripture, having been taught well by their mother. It's also here we learn the boys' names are James, Joseph, Samuel, and Matthew.

While at the palace, a man named Mr. Brisk, who only pretends to be religious, attempts to woo Mercy. He believes the young woman would make an excellent housewife, but when Mercy rejects his offers, he spreads nasty rumors about her. While still at the palace, Christiana's oldest son, Matthew, becomes violently ill from eating the fruit from the trees in the devil's orchard earlier on the Way. They call for a doctor named Mr. Skill, who administers pills to be taken with fasting and tears of repentance. The treatment is successful, and Matthew gets better.

As the group travels down the hill into the Valley of Humiliation, Great Heart shows them the place where Christian slipped and fell just prior to battle with the notorious beast, Apollyon.

Having safely passed through that valley, they enter the dark and desert-like Valley of the Shadow of Death. It's there they hear a considerable amount of groaning, like that of dying men, and encounter another giant, named Maul. The giant accuses Great Heart of kidnapping the women and children, and after a tough battle, Great Heart defeats Maul and fastens the giant's head on an inscribed pillar as a message to others passing by.

Leaving the valley, the pilgrims meet a man named Honest, whom they soon recognize to be a pilgrim traveling to the Celestial City. He joins their group, and he and Great Heart discuss Mr. Fearing, a mutual friend who made it to the Celestial City but only after much struggle. They also discuss another man, named Mr. Self Will, who claimed to be a pilgrim but never succeeded in his journey.

The pilgrims soon grow weary and need rest. Based on a recommendation from Honest, they go to the home of an old disciple, named Gaius. The innkeeper is a wise man who welcomes them into his home, where they stay for a month. Gaius tells them of a local menacing giant named Slay Good who endangers pilgrims on the Way. Great Heart assembles a group to search for the giant and eventually finds him tormenting a hostage named Mr. Feeble Mind. They kill Slay Good and rescue Feeble Mind, bringing him back to the inn and adding him to their group. Before leaving the inn, Matthew and Mercy are married, and Gaius's daughter is married to James. They also meet a handicapped man named Ready-to-halt, who joins their group as a companion for Feeble Mind.

Next, the pilgrims arrive at the town of Vanity, where Great Heart leads them to Mr. Mnason's house. They stay for many years in Vanity, where Mnason's daughters Grace and Martha marry Samuel and Joseph, respectively. Also while there, a great monster comes out of the woods and kills many of the townsfolk as well as capturing children from the town. Great Heart assembles a group of men who wound the beast and, as a result, saves the town. The men become heroes, leaving Vanity in a much better state than Christian and Faithful did.

The pilgrims leave Vanity and pass the silver mine where By-ends fell in and died as well as the salt-pillar monument erected to turn men away from sin. Eventually they come to the field that lies before the Delectable Mountains, and Christiana advises her four daughters to commit their little ones to the responsibility of the Man there who cares for the lambs.

They continue their journey, arriving at By-path Meadow, and see the fence where Christian and Hopeful had crossed over. Great Heart and the men decide to go to Doubting Castle to free any pilgrims trapped there. The men successfully slay Giant Despair and his wife, Dissident, and free Mr. Despondence and his daughter, Much-afraid, from the giant's dungeon.

The pilgrims reach the Delectable Mountains, where they meet a group of shepherds who show them everything that was shown to Christian plus more wonders of the land. The shepherds give each of the women a gift from the house but do not provide a map of their remaining journey as they had to Christian and Hopeful, since Christiana's group has Great Heart as their guide.

As they near the Celestial City, they encounter a badly beaten pilgrim named Valiant-for-Truth, who has just fended off an attack in the same place where Little Faith was robbed. Great Heart invites the brave warrior to join their group. With a new warrior at their side, they pass through the Enchanted Ground. Even though they desire rest, Great Heart wisely presses them forward, aided by his map that details the way to the Celestial City.

As they reach the end of the Enchanted Ground, they encounter a man named Standfast, who, through prayer, has overcome the temptations of Madam Bubble. Adding him to their growing group, they head to the Land of Beulah.

Arriving in Beulah, their now large group comes to the River of Death. Christiana is the first to cross over, followed by the others. However, Christiana's boys and their wives remain behind to help grow the church left on Earth.

Character Summary

THE NARRATOR

The narrator is an anonymous person, most likely John Bunyan, who is wandering in the wilderness then lays down in a clearing to sleep. In the first *Pilgrim's Progress*, he dreams of the story of a pilgrim named Christian and his adventures on the Way to the Celestial City. In the sequel, he dreams of Christian's wife, Christiana, and their four boys as they begin the same journey.

CHRISTIAN

Christian is the protagonist of the first book who flees his hometown, the City of Destruction, for fear that God is going to destroy it. He carries a heavy burden on his back, representing the fears for his own soul, so he leaves his family to journey to the Celestial City in search of a cure for his burden. Along the way, he meets various characters who either bring him closer to his goal or lead him off the path.

CHRISTIANA

Christiana is the wife of Christian, who initially mocks her husband for wanting to go on a pilgrimage and refuses to go with him. After his death, she experiences vivid memories of Christian's suffering and agony. Now filled with guilt herself for dismissing him as insane, she, too, battles those same feelings that Christian did under the weight of her own burden of sin. Awakened to the realities of sin and judgment in their own lives, she and her children leave the City of Destruction and began a pilgrimage of their own.

THE BOYS (Matthew, James, Samuel, and Joseph)

Christian and Christiana's children began as boys at the beginning of the story and grow to men by the end. The oldest, Matthew, is married to Mercy; James marries Phebe; Samuel marries Grace; and Joseph marries Martha.

MERCY

Mercy is a young woman who is touched by the sincerity of her neighbor Christiana's faith and joins them on their journey. She was not called directly by God but pleads at the Wicket Gate for entrance and is graciously admitted because her heart is true and her faith is earnest. Eventually she marries Christiana's eldest son, Matthew.

MR. SAGACITY

In Bunyan's dream, Mr. Sagacity informs the narrator of all that has happened since Christian's departure and how Christian's wife, Christiana, and the boys were initially devastated but had second thoughts and have packed up to follow his path to the Celestial City.

SECRET

Secret is a heavenly messenger sent to Christiana to present her with a letter from the King saying that He forgives her and invites her to come to Him in the Celestial City.

MRS. NEVROUSNESS

Mrs. Nervousness is the daughter of the man Christian met on the Hill of Difficulty, who told him to go back for fear of the lions. She, too, tries to deter Christiana from leaving the City of Destruction using fear tactics.

THE RELIEVER

The Reliever lives at the gate, and he rescues Christiana and Mercy from being attacked by two wicked men.

THE INTERPRETER

The Interpreter, representing the Holy Spirit, lives in a large house where pilgrims stop for instructions, for guidance, and to become equipped in allegorical understanding. He instructs pilgrims by showing them a series of vignettes, each with a hidden religious meaning, helping them eventually learn to interpret the signs for themselves.

GREAT HEART

Great Heart is a guide sent by the Interpreter to direct, guide, and protect the pilgrims along the Way to the Celestial City. He represents the pastor of a church, and without him, their journey would have been more difficult.

GRIM (BLOODY-MAN)

Grim, also known as Bloody-man because he has killed many pilgrims, is a giant the pilgrims meet just prior to arriving at the Palace Beautiful. He was there to support the lions, who were fully awake as the pilgrims were passing through.

WATCHFUL

Watchful is the porter at the Palace Beautiful and is the overseer of the palace who stands guard to make sure that only genuine believers come in.

THE FOUR SISTERS OF THE PALACE BEAUTIFUL

The four sisters of the Palace Beautiful (Discretion, Prudence, Piety, and Charity) help passing pilgrims find their way on the path.

MR. BRISK

Mr. Brisk is Mercy's suitor while the pilgrims are visiting the Palace Beautiful. He pretends to be religious to woo her, but after she rejects his offer, he spreads nasty rumors about her.

MR. SKILL

Mr. Skill is the physician summoned to heal Matthew after the fruit from the devil's orchard makes him sick.

MAUL

Maul is another giant the pilgrims meet toward the end of the Valley of the Shadow of Death. He accuses Great Heart of kidnapping the women and children and is in the habit of offering deceptive and flawed philosophies to passing pilgrims.

MR. HONEST

The pilgrims encounter Mr. Honest coming out of the Valley of the Shadow of Death. He is a fellow pilgrim and the first outsider to join the traveling group.

MR. FEARING

Mr. Fearing is a mutual acquaintance of Great Heart and Honest, albeit a very troubled man, who displays a crippling fear of death and hell, as well as offending others, but eventually gets to heaven.

MR. SELF WILL

Mr. Self Will claimed to be a pilgrim but never succeeded in his journey because he used his own interpretation of Scripture to justify his continued sinful behavior.

GAIUS

Gaius is a generous innkeeper who welcomes the pilgrims into his home and feeds them while providing wisdom and instruction. His daughter, Phebe, marries Christiana's son James.

MR. FEEBLE MIND

After Mr. Feeble Mind is captured by the giant Slay Good and cannot fight back, Great Heart rescues him and brings him into the company of the other pilgrims.

SLAY GOOD

The giant Slay Good is a local menace who torments pilgrims along the Way. Great Heart and his band of pilgrims defeat him in battle and free Feeble Mind.

MR. MNASON

Mr. Mnason is Great Heart's friend who lives in Vanity. He welcomes the pilgrims into his home and introduces them to other good men in town. They stay for many years in Vanity, where Mnason's daughters Grace and Martha marry Samuel and Joseph, respectively.

GIANT DESPAIR

Giant Despair is the master at Doubting Castle and imprisons pilgrims who trespass on his property. He represents the temptation of despair and depression that results when we do not manage the conviction of our sin biblically.

MR. DESPONDENCY AND MUCH-AFRAID

Mr. Despondency and his daughter, Much-afraid, were prisoners in Doubting Castle and trapped by Giant Despair. Great Heart and others rescue them and add them to the pilgrim's' group.

VALIANT-FOR-TRUTH

Valiant-for-Truth is a pilgrim whom Great Heart and the others find bloody and beaten, having just battled attackers in the same place where Little Faith was robbed. Impressed with the man's courage and strength, Great Heart invites him to join them to help with the weaker members of the group.

STANDFAST

Standfast is a pilgrim who, through prayer, overcomes the machinations of Madam Bubble, the witch of the Enchanted Ground. He joins the group at the end of their journey.

MADAM BUBBLE

Madam Bubble is the witch who enchants the Enchanted Ground and represents the world's temptations.

THE SHEPHERDS

The Shepherds (Knowledge, Experience, and Watchful) live on the Delectable Mountains, just on the edge of the Enchanted Grounds. They provide support, education, and warnings for pilgrims as they begin the last leg of their journey.

Places Summary

CITY OF DESTRUCTION

The City of Destruction is Christian and Christiana's hometown and is a symbol of the entire world, with all its sins, corruptions, and sorrow and with no hope of salvation.

SWAMP OF DESPAIR

The Swamp of Despair is the first major obstacle the pilgrims face on their way to the Wicket Gate. Here, pilgrims are likely to become so overwhelmed with conviction over their sin that they enter a state of depression and discouragement and get bogged down and trapped in the mud.

THE WICKET GATE

The Wicket Gate is the only entrance to the Way and puts pilgrims on the narrow path to the Celestial City. The gate represents Christ, and passing through it represents one's conversion.

THE HOUSE OF THE INTERPRETER

The House of the Interpreter has many rooms where pilgrims learn many metaphorical lessons about their new faith that spur them into religious thinking.

THE CROSS

The Cross is located on higher ground, and at the foot of it is a tomb. In the first book, when Christian approaches the Cross, the burden on his back rolls off and into the tomb.

THE HILL OF DIFFICULTY

The Hill of Difficulty stands between pilgrims and the Palace Beautiful and must be climbed to get there. The hill represents many things in the life of a believer, including opposition, persecution, temptations, physical difficulties, overcoming sinful habits, forgiveness, etc.

THE PALACE BEAUTIFUL

The Palace Beautiful is at the top of the Hill of Difficulty and is where four sisters live (Discretion, Prudence, Piety, and Charity). They examine the consciences of passing pilgrims and provide them shelter and supplies for their journey, including a suit of armor if they do not have a guide.

THE VALLEY OF HUMILIATION

The Valley of Humiliation is at the bottom of the Hill of Difficulty and metaphorically is when we throw down our pride and recognize we are nothing without God.

THE VALLEY OF THE SHADOW OF DEATH

The Valley of the Shadow of Death is a darker and more sinister place than the Valley of Humiliation. When pilgrims proceed through this dark and desert-like valley that's haunted by demons, they find their best defense is prayer. The Valley of the Shadow of Death represents the trials, temptations, and tribulations we go through in the Christian life.

VANITY FAIR

Vanity Fair is a wicked town that hosts a year-long carnival designed to tempt pilgrims to abandon their journeys. Unlike Christian and Faithful's experience in the town, Christiana and her group encounter a small church when they arrive and stay there for many years.

DOUBTING CASTLE

Doubting Castle is located off the narrow Way that pilgrims often take when they think they have found an easier path. Its master is Giant Despair, and he and his wife, Diffidence, capture, imprison, and torture pilgrims. The dungeon of Doubting Castle is a miserable, unforgiving place, representing the doubts and fears of those that feel trapped under the weight of their sin.

THE DELECTABLE MOUNTAINS

The Delectable Mountains contain gardens, orchards, vineyards, and fountains of water. There are four shepherds who live there (Experience, Knowledge, Watchful, and Sincere) who show pilgrims a variety of wonders, provide them with a map to avoid traps along the Way, and warn them to beware of the Flatterer.

THE ENCHANTED GROUND

The Enchanted Ground is a place where, if pilgrims fall asleep, they might never wake. It represents a time in our lives when things are going relatively well, leaving us spiritually complacent.

THE COUNTRY OF BEULAH

The Country of Beulah is a place of safety that borders Heaven and is within sight of the Celestial City, where angels commonly walk. It is a land of abundant provision and far beyond the reach of the temptations of this life. In the sequel, it's the last stop where pilgrims await their summons to cross the River of Death.

THE RIVER OF DEATH

The River of Death is a deep and foreboding river that pilgrims must cross to reach the gate of the Celestial City. The depth of the river changes to reflect the doubt or faith of the person who enters it.

THE CELESTIAL CITY

The Celestial City on Mount Zion, or Heaven, is the final destination for all pilgrims. Once admitted through the gate by the King, or God, they are surrounded by a choir of angels with trumpet fanfares and welcomed by the joyous celebration of its residents.

Session 1: Leaving the City of Destruction

In this week's readings, Bunyan comes to us again as the narrator of his own dream, reporting back to his readers regarding the fate of Christian's wife, Christiana, and their four boys. The story begins with an encounter with Mr. Sagacity, who informs him that Christiana and her sons have left the City of Destruction and set out on their own pilgrimage to the Celestial City. Since the death of her husband, Christiana has become overwhelmed with conviction regarding her treatment of Christian before he left on his own pilgrimage. Now she, too, feels the weight and burden of her own sin and receives a royal letter from the King. In the letter, He forgives Christiana and desires her to come into His presence by following the same journey Christian took. Despite discouragement from a neighbor, Christiana and the boys prepare to leave, taking a young neighbor woman, Mercy, with them to the Wicket Gate, where they will begin their journey on the Way.

Session 1 Chapters

Answer Guide and Scripture References Available at www.BrownChairBooks.com

---

Chapter 1: Mr. Sagacity

1. The definition of sagacity is having the qualities of wisdom, intelligence, and discernment and the ability to make good judgments. Mr. Sagacity enters Bunyan's dream representing the wisdom needed to journey through this world. He stands in stark contrast to Worldly Wiseman, who offered ungodly counsel to Christian in the first book. What characteristics do you look for when seeking counsel from another for major life decisions?

2. What areas of your life are the easiest to trust God with? Which is the most difficult? Read Proverbs 19:20–21. Why is having a heart that's surrendered to God essential when seeking godly counsel?

3. Mr. Sagacity claims Christian had many the adoring fan of his adventures to the Celestial City, but few were "resolved enough to run the same risks that he did." Sagacity seems to allude to those that sit on the fence of Christianity, never realizing the devil owns the fence. According to Matthew 12:30, what did Jesus say are the only two possible relationships with God? Some people might say that they are all in with Jesus but ride the fence on certain issues that they have a hard time reconciling in their minds. What do you think some of these issues might be, and is it possible to ride the fence here?

Chapter 2: Christiana and Her Boys

1. Explain why you think Christiana is completely overwhelmed with guilt, shame, and conviction. Do you harbor any regrets or sorrow over any unresolved treatment of another from your past? How have you dealt with it thus far?

2. Many people live paralyzed with regret over memories of wrongs they've committed against others. What instruction does Jesus offer us in Matthew 5:23–24 when we remember those regrets? Read 2 Corinthians 7:10 and Philippians 3:13. How might these two passages suggest a model for handling the hurt we've caused others that may have died or are utterly inaccessible?

3. It pleases Christiana to receive her invitation from the King to come to the Celestial City, but she wonders if Secret might just carry them directly there, in other words, bypass the journey. What was Secret's response? Becoming a Christian does not guarantee a peaceful life. In fact, Jesus makes it clear in John 16:1–4 and verse 33 that life is full of trouble and following Him can lead to persecution. Why might some new believers think accepting Jesus leads to a prosperous life with few or no problems?

Chapter 3: A Conversation with Mrs. Nervousness

1. Christiana was antagonistic toward her husband before he left on a pilgrimage. Now she is experiencing the same treatment from her neighbor, Mrs. Nervousness. Read 2 Corinthians 2:14–16. Why do some people respond not only with indifference but with outright antagonism toward those seeking God? How should we respond to those who try to dampen our spiritual interest?

2. Mrs. Nervousness is the daughter of the man Christian met on the Hill of Difficulty, who told him to go back for fear of the lions ahead. There are common sayings concerning generational relationships, like "He's a chip off the old block," "Like father, like son," and "The apple doesn't fall far from the tree." But there are also behavioral patterns that are learned, like alcoholism, poor work ethic, anger issues, and even fear. Exodus 34:6–7 describes sin that's not just passed down but also willingly accepted through generations. What generational sin patterns in your own family are you aware of? Describe any efforts you've made to break those patterns. How has your faith been instrumental in those efforts?

3. Mercy is attracted to Christiana's passion for leaving on a pilgrimage and reaching her King in the Celestial City. Read Romans 12:11. What do you think it means to be fervent in spirit? What would your life look like if you were more fervent in spirit?

Chapter 4: The Wicket Gate

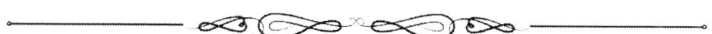

1. Mercy becomes upset thinking about the family she's leaving behind in the City of Destruction. Christiana offers her hope, explaining that Christian also left her and the boys behind, but here they are now, heading on a pilgrimage. She believes this was in large part due to Christian's continual prayers for his family. Psalm 56:8 says that God hears, answers, and even stores up our prayers. What comfort might this verse bring to you when praying for someone that you may never see come to Christ in your lifetime?

2. The Swamp of Despair represents a time in one's life when they become so overwhelmed with conviction over sin that they enter a state of depression and discouragement. They might also experience fears, doubts, anxieties, and hopelessness. The swamp also represents temptation, pride, and other transgressions, both open and secret, that keep us down. Christiana comes to a standstill at the swamp as she recalls her own guilt and shame about her treatment of Christian. Describe a time in your life when shame or depression paralyzed you from moving any further, and mention any who encouraged you as Mercy did for Christiana.

3. They arrive at the Wicket Gate, and like her husband, Christiana knocks many times to be let in. Read Matthew 7:13–14. What does the gate represent? Read Matthew 7:7–8. What does the knocking teach us about man's responsibility in salvation?

Chapter 5: Intercession for Mercy

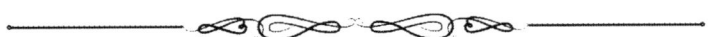

1. When Christiana and her sons enter the gate, they leave Mercy alone outside. From the beginning, Mercy had feared they would not receive her at the gate, and now it appears those fears are coming true. Christiana, though, doesn't rest in her own blessed state but intercedes for her friend. What does 1 Timothy 2:1–4 say about a Christian's responsibility for intercessory prayer?

2. Mercy suddenly panics outside the gate, wondering if Christiana is inside interceding on her behalf. She knows she can't turn back or wait any longer, so she knocks so loudly that it startles Christiana. When the gate keeper looks out, he finds Mercy has fainted. Mercy represents those who feel that—for whatever reason—God won't save them. Who is Jesus praying for in John 17:20? Why is this good news for Mercy and others that truly desire grace and forgiveness but struggle to believe God can or will save them?

3. When trying to reach the gate, Christian faced flaming arrows, while Christiana's group faces a ferocious dog owned by Satan. Both represent the opposition one might face when coming to Christ. What specific opposition might one face when they are on the threshold of salvation?

Session 2: Following Christian

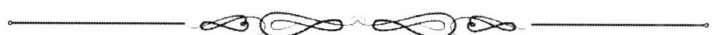

In this week's readings, the women and children continue their journey, leaving the comfort and safety of the gate to begin their journey on the Way. Having not been on the path long, Christiana chastises the boys for mischievously eating fruit from the devil's orchard. Then two wicked men attack them, only for Christiana and Mercy to be rescued by the Reliever from a nearby house, who wonders why Christiana did not ask for a guide. They next arrive at the house of the Interpreter, who shows the women various meaningful scenes in his Significant Rooms, just as he did before with Christian. They travel past the cross and tomb and then up the Hill of Difficulty, where they learn the fates of Simple, Lazy, Arrogance, Formalism, and Hypocrisy.

Session 2 Chapters

Chapter 6: Distracted from Danger
Chapter 7: The Interpreter's House
Chapter 8: Great Heart Leads the Women
Chapter 9: The Consequences of the Cross
Chapter 10: Following the Path of Christian

Chapter 6: Distracted from Danger

1. Entering through the gate and onto the Way, Christiana is so focused on the blessings received at the gate that she becomes distracted from the imminent dangers of the road. What dangers does she place the entire group in, and what earlier steps could she have taken to prevent it? Read 1 Peter 5:8. How is comparing Satan to a roaring lion accurate? In what ways do we let our spiritual guard down when all seems to be going well?

2. When attacked by two wicked men, Christiana and Mercy respond appropriately. First, they cover themselves, then they stand their ground and try to continue their journey. They fiercely resist the attack, and when unable to run, they call for help. The attackers represent our sinful nature, which is intent on destroying both "body and soul." Consider each defense the women employed in fending off the attacks. How might these apply to your own struggle with sin?

3. The Reliever tells the group that the gate keeper would have sent a guide to escort them if they had asked. Since they did not ask, they did not receive. Is Matthew 7:7 a blanket promise with no conditions?

Chapter 7: The Interpreter's House

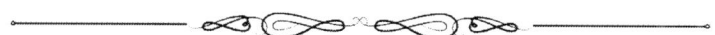

1. Christiana, Mercy, and the boys arrive at the Interpreter's house. The Interpreter represents the Holy Spirit, who, once we profess Christ, sheds light on the Scriptures to help us better understand how we should relate to God, other people, and the world lest we remain in darkness. Just as the Interpreter did with Christian, he shows the pilgrims a wide variety of metaphors. The first scene is a man raking leaves and twigs, who is oblivious to the One standing overhead, offering him a Celestial Crown. What does the man with the muck–rake represent? How might a believer's life change if they were to truly offer the prayer found in Proverbs 30:8?

2. Next the Interpreter takes them to one of the best rooms in the house, which is home to a spider. This metaphor is to teach them two things: First, sin is still present in a Christian's life, and however small it is, it's dangerous, like the venom of a spider. Second, like a spider clinging to a wall, we, too, should be resilient in our faith, clinging to Christ. In 1 Timothy 1:19, Paul charges Timothy to cling to his faith and keep his conscience clear, doing what he knows is right. What does having a good conscience have to do with keeping the faith? What is the danger of failing to keep a clear conscience? How does Paul describe it?

3. What do the pilgrims notice about the robin in the garden, and what warning does the robin represent? Read Matthew 7:23. How can some people believe they are Christians when, in fact, they are not? What does James 2:18 say about true faith?

Chapter 8: Great Heart Leads the Women

1. As they await dinner, the Interpreter asks both Christiana and Mercy to share their testimonies. How does each woman approach her own story of repentance? Read 1 Peter 3:15–16. When someone asks you why you believe in Christ, how do you respond? Are you ready to give them an answer with gentleness and respect? Take some time to write out how you would respond to the question if asked.

2. The next morning, the group is bathed and clothed in white, with a seal placed on their foreheads. There are obvious ceremonial references here to baptism combined with end times prophecy. Bunyan also focuses on the beauty that both Christiana and Mercy see in the other. In Philippians 2:3–4, Paul describes how the measure of our own spiritual journey might be in how we view others. Why is it so difficult to think of others as better than yourself? What are some reasons that we struggle to live with such humility? What can you do to shift your focus toward taking an interest in others?

3. In the first book, Christian fights most of his battles on his own, with occasional help. In the sequel, we see the value of a community of believers led by a servant–warrior pastor. Great Heart represents this pastor as the heroic defender and guide who escorts the pilgrims along the Way. What servant–warrior pastor have you known who slays the giants of this world with the Word and warns his people of imminent dangers? What are some traits of Great Heart pastors?

Chapter 9: The Consequences of the Cross

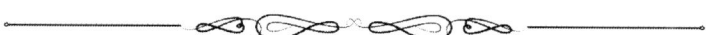

1. Seeing the cross reminded Christiana of the promise of forgiveness, but she still didn't understand how it was accomplished by Christ. Great Heart explained that there's nobody else like Jesus Christ, who is both human and divine, who possessed enough righteousness for everyone and needed none for Himself. Read Philippians 2:5–7 and Hebrews 4:15–16. Is it difficult for you to believe Jesus Christ, a man, also existed in the form of God? What does it matter that Christ was both fully man and fully God?

2. What was Great Heart's response as to whether Christian understood this teaching when he leaped for joy after the burden rolled off his shoulders at the cross? Besides offering comfort and easing our burden of sin, what else did Great Heart say happens when we understand and accept this teaching? According to Romans 5:8–11, what did God's love for us cost Him, and what should be our response to that love?

3. Affected by the thought of Christ's sacrifice on the cross, Christiana believes that her neighbors back in the City of Destruction would undergo the same change of heart she has if they could understand what Christ has done for them. What does this say about Christiana's heart but also her naiveté? What's wrong with thinking that if people are just exposed to the love of Jesus Christ, they will repent and turn to Him?

Chapter 10: Following the Path of Christian

1. Continuing on the Way, the pilgrims see that Simple, Lazy, and Arrogance were all hanged and punished. In what ways did these men hinder others and try to persuade them away from their pilgrimages? These men represent false teachers that Paul mentions in Galatians 5:7, who were pulling believers away from the truth of the gospel. What in your life causes you to stumble or pulls you away from believing and knowing the truth of God's love for you?

2. At the foot of the Hill of Difficulty, the group discovers the deadly paths that Formality and Hypocrisy had followed now blocked off. But even with all the chains, posts, and a ditch, some travelers still chose those paths because they did not want to ascend the hill—to their own peril. How did these trespassers respond when warned? In Jeremiah 44:16–17, the kidnapped prophet was in Egypt but continued to warn the disobedient Israelites of their sin. We might paraphrase their response to him this way: "We will not listen. We will not obey. We reject God's warning. We will continue doing as we please." How do you see this same type of disobedience playing out in culture today?

3. Christiana's group starts up the hill, but in the hot sun, the pilgrims grow weary. Great Heart urges them onward until they reach the Prince's Arbor, about halfway up the hill, where they rest. Read Psalm 23:1–3 and Matthew 11:28. What does the shady arbor represent in the life of a Christian? How were the pilgrims refreshed at the arbor?

Session 3: Challenges Along the Way

In this week's readings, although equipped for their journey and thankful for the guidance of Great Heart, the pilgrims soon meet challenges along the Way. The fierce lions that were asleep when Christian passed by are now awake and assisted by a gruesome giant named Grim. Fearing for their lives, the pilgrims watch their brave guide defeat the giant, allowing them to pass without incident. Great Heart then guides them to the Palace Beautiful, where the sisters invite them to stay for a month to learn more about their faith from those inside the house. One sister, Prudence, examines each boy's faith, providing an opportunity for each boy to share their testimony and explain what they believe. Mercy grows in discernment after fending off a potential suitor, who, once spurned by her rejection, begins to spread nasty rumors about her. And when her son, Matthew, almost dies because of a poor decision he made, Christiana's faith grows as a parent dealing with the consequences of a rebellious child.

Session 3 Chapters

Chapter 11: An Encounter with Grim
Chapter 12: Arrival at the Palace Beautiful
Chapter 13: Prudence Talks to the Boys About Faith
Chapter 14: Mr. Brisk Visits Mercy
Chapter 15: Matthew Falls Sick

Chapter 11: An Encounter with Grim

1. On their way to the Palace Beautiful (representing the church), the pilgrims come upon the spot where Mistrust and Nervousness tried to warn Christian off from the lions and were severely punished for having interfered in his journey. These two men represent those that use deception to dissuade believers from church but can also represent our own fears of attending church. What anxieties or fears might keep people from church? How does Paul challenge us in 2 Corinthians 10:5 to control the daily thoughts that enter our minds, and how do we take every thought captive?

2. As the pilgrims draw near the palace, they notice the grass has overgrown the path, leading them to believe that few pilgrims have passed near the lions recently. When told by Giant Grim to turn back, Christiana makes a bold stand, harkening back to the stand Deborah, the judge and prophetess or Israel, made against the oppression of the Canaanites in Judges 5–6. What can we learn from the stance Deborah took in the battle against Israel's enemies? What role did she play? What role did God play?

3. Grim can't believe Great Heart would kill him on his own ground. But Great Heart rebukes him, claiming it's the King's road and it's Grim who is trespassing. Read Ephesians 4:27. Identify some of the primary ways in your own life that you secede ground to the devil. In what other ways, perhaps that seem minor and unobtrusive but could have major ramifications, are you allowing the devil room?

Chapter 12: Arrival at the Palace Beautiful

1. When Christiana's group arrives at the Palace Beautiful, Great Heart tells them he must leave and return to the Interpreter's house. The group begs him to stay for encouragement and protection, but his task was only to bring them this far. Reading Titus 1:5, we can only imagine Paul's young mentee begging his mentor to stay in Crete to help with a struggling church. What were Paul's reasons for leaving, and how might this have helped Titus grow in his faith? How might a Christian mentor know when to pull back for the benefit of their mentee?

2. Though the pilgrims are exhausted and eager for rest and sleep, the family in the palace encourages them to eat first. Metaphorically, Bunyan uses specific foods that allude to the Passover meal, perhaps representing the first Lord's Supper for Christians. Jesus commands us in Luke 22:19 to take part in the supper in remembrance of Him. How might the Lord's Supper rejuvenate our hearts when spiritually exhausted, as these pilgrims were? When you partake of and meditate on the Lord's Supper, which part is most meaningful for you at this point in your spiritual journey?

3. The next morning, Christiana asks Mercy why she was laughing in her sleep. Mercy shares a dream she had about an angel bringing her to heaven, where she saw Christian. Christiana believes such dreams are a sign from God and that God can speak to the heart even when a person is asleep. In the Bible, there are several places where dreams play a role in advancing the story of God's people. Do you think that God still speaks through dreams today? How do you balance a dream you believe is from God and the authority of Scripture?

Chapter 13: Prudence Talks to the Boys About Faith

1. Christiana and her companions remain at the Palace Beautiful for about a month, during which time Prudence instructs Christiana's four sons in question-and-answer sessions about Christian doctrines, the Holy Ghost, the value of the Bible, and the nature of heaven and hell. If you're a parent or grandparent, rate yourself between 1 and 10 on how well you teach your children or grandchildren about Christian doctrine. Why did you choose that rating? Why do you think so many Christian parents outsource basic Christian teaching to someone else?

2. Read 2 Timothy 1:5 and 3:14–17. What does Paul remember about Timothy's family and spiritual background? How does Paul describe Timothy's faith? Do you have anyone like this in your faith background? If so, describe this person and how they influenced your faith. How might these verses encourage parents today who feel like they are fighting a losing battle?

3. Christiana's education of the boys impresses Prudence, as they all appear well versed in their faith. She encourages them to continue listening to their mother, as she has much more to teach them. Read Ephesians 6:1–3. What is the promise that is associated with this command? How does obedience relate to having a good life and living long? Describe the social problems that result from disobedience in the home.

Chapter 14: Mr. Brisk Visits Mercy

1. After a week at the Palace Beautiful, a man named Mr. Brisk courts the attractive and industrious Mercy and is interested in marrying her. However, the other women in the house alert Mercy that he only pretends to be religious. What are some problems that can arise in a marriage between a believer and an unbeliever? What marriages have you seen struggle because of an unbelieving spouse?

2. Heeding the advice of godly friends, Mercy successfully wards off the unwanted attention of Mr. Brisk as he loses interest when he learns she makes clothes for the poor rather than for profit. Read 2 Corinthians 6:14–16. What strong language does Paul use to warn believers of uniting with non-Christian influences in their lives? What dangers are clearest in these types of relationships?

3. Prudence warns Mercy that Brisk might slander her because of her rejection of him. But Mercy is strong in her decision to refuse him and vows never to compromise her principles for any man, even if it means dying an old maid. Too often we believe it's okay to compromise our faith, our belief system, and our moral values for the sake of getting what we think we deserve in life. How far were Shadrach, Meshach, and Abednego willing to go so as not to compromise their faith in Daniel 3:16–18? According to Psalm 1:1, how can we avoid spiritual compromise in this present age and time?

Chapter 15: Matthew Falls Sick

1. While they are still at the palace, Matthew, Christiana's oldest son, falls ill because of the forbidden fruit he ate just after coming through the Wicket Gate. They summon an old physician named Dr. Skill, who diagnoses Matthew with severe gastric pain and declares he will die unless his stomach is purged. Read Proverbs 19:20–21. What two things are key to being counted among the wise? As with Matthew eating the fruit, sometimes the disastrous effects of not accepting wise counsel and discipline are delayed. Can you identify an area of your life where you didn't seek godly counsel and suffered the consequences later in life?

2. Dr. Skill prepares a medicine called *ex carne et sanguine Christi* ("from the body and blood of Christ") to be taken with fasting and repentance. Read King David's confession in Psalm 32:3–5. How did David respond to the Lord's "heavy hand" on him? How did God motivate David to confess his sin? What did David experience after he confessed his sin to God? How did God respond to David's confession?

3. As Matthew recovers, Christiana purchases several boxes of the pills to hedge against diseases that the pilgrims are likely to face on their journey. Dr. Skill is happy to oblige, saying it's a universal pill that will cure anything. However, he is insistent they take the medicine exactly as prescribed. According to Luke 13:3, is there forgiveness from God without repentance? Have you ever tried to get over a sin in your life without repenting? Explain.

Session 4: The Path Through the Valleys

In this week's readings, Great Heart returns to the Palace Beautiful to escort the pilgrims back on the Way. They travel down into the valleys, beginning with the Valley of Humiliation, and find the place where Christian defeated Apollyon. Having safely passed through that valley, they next enter through the Valley of the Shadow of Death. There they encounter the giant Maul, who accuses Great Heart of kidnapping the women and children. With the giant slayed, they leave the valley and meet another traveling pilgrim, Mr. Honest, who joins their group. As they continue journeying along the Way, they discuss Mr. Fearing, a mutual friend of both Honest and Great Heart. They also discuss another man, Mr. Self Will, who claimed to be a pilgrim but never succeeded in his journey.

Session 4 Chapters

Chapter 16: Leaving the Palace Beautiful
Chapter 17: The Valley of Humiliation
Chapter 18: The Valley of the Shadow of Death
Chapter 19: Old Honest and Mr. Fearing
Chapter 20: Mr. Self Will

Chapter 16: Leaving the Palace Beautiful

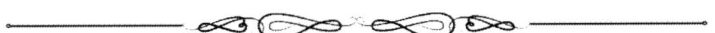

1. After a month in the Palace Beautiful, it's time for Christiana and her group to leave. As with Christian before them, the family of the palace sends them off with sights of some special objects. First they show the pilgrims the apple Eve ate and gave to Adam that resulted in their expulsion from Paradise. What did Christiana think the apple was, and why might she have been confused? Read 2 Corinthians 11:14–15. What does it mean that Satan masquerades as an angel of light? According to Psalm 119:105 and 119:130, how can we discern which light is of God and which light is of Satan?

2. Next they give Christiana a golden anchor and tell her it's essential for her to hold on to it in case they encounter turbulent weather. Why do our souls need an anchor? In Hebrews 6:17–20, how does the writer describe the hope a believer has in Jesus, and what does he base this hope on? Describe a time when God's promises kept your hope anchored during a difficult storm.

3. As they leave, Christiana hears birds singing. Prudence references Song of Solomon 2:11–12, explaining that the birds only sing in the spring, when the flowers appear. In C. S. Lewis's *The Lion, the Witch, and the Wardrobe*, the White Witch cast her spell on Narnia, decreeing it must always be winter and never Christmas. Then Aslan shows up and breaks the witch's power, and the snow begins to melt. What powerful winter/springtime metaphor are both Bunyan and Lewis suggesting in relation to the life of a believer?

Chapter 17: The Valley of Humiliation

1. As the pilgrims carefully make their way down into the Valley of Humiliation, they find it much more pleasant than Christian did; for him, it was a place of intense spiritual warfare, fear, and torment. Great Heart explains that the valley is not a haunted place but a beautiful, fruitful, and peaceful place well suited to contemplation. Why does Great Heart suggest we might not recognize it as a beautiful place? How does Paul suggest we maintain an appropriate level of humility in 2 Corinthians 12:7–10? What kind of experiences have you had in the Valley of Humiliation?

2. Bunyan's metaphorical use of the Valley of Humiliation appears to reflect a state of mind and the quality of our hearts and spirits before the Lord. Great Heart claims that no one willingly walks through the valley unless they love the Lord. If the path of the Christian runs through the Valley of Humiliation, why is it such a struggle? According to Philippians 2:8, how did Christ exemplify genuine humility? Read James 4:6. Why should we embrace the Valley of Humiliation?

3. Great Heart points out a spot on the path called Forgetful Green, where Christian's battle with Apollyon took place. What is this place, and why is it so dangerous for Christians? In this book, the pilgrims see many monuments that mark Christian's journey and even set up some of their own. Why is it important to mark the blessings you have received from the Lord?

Chapter 18: The Valley of the Shadow of Death

1. The Valley of the Shadow of Death represents the trials, temptations, and tribulations we go through in the Christian life. It's a dangerous, dark place, where one encounters heightened spiritual opposition. The pilgrims enter the valley, catching frequent glimpses of evil creatures, hearing the groanings of dead men and snakes hissing, and feeling the earth shake. In what ways are we vulnerable in the valley? What simple truth about this valley should we remember in Psalm 23:4, and how does Paul rephrase 2 Corinthians 4:8–9?

2. As the pilgrims proceed through the valley, they are terrified, first by a fiend approaching them and then by a roaring lion behind them. Both times Great Heart prepares for battle, and both times the enemy flees. It reminds Christiana of James 4:7: "Resist the devil, and he will flee from you." What does it mean to resist the devil? Why are the first lines of this verse—"Submit yourselves, then, to God"—perhaps the most important part?

3. Before leaving the valley, Giant Maul attempts to trick the pilgrims into thinking Great Heart has kidnapped them. The long ensuing battle between Great Heart and Maul reminds us of the difficulty of dismantling and vanquishing arguments, especially those that appear to have some credence. John 8:44 says the devil is a liar. According to 2 Corinthians 10:5, how can we identify the common lies of the devil in our lives and fight back?

Chapter 19: Old Honest and Mr. Fearing

1. Emerging from the Valley of the Shadow of Death, the pilgrims meet an older pilgrim named Honest from the town of Stupidity, where the people are frozen and senseless unless the Sun of Righteousness shines on them. Martin Luther King Jr. said, "Nothing in all the world is more dangerous than sincere ignorance and conscientious stupidity." In Jeremiah 4:22, how did the prophet describe the people of Judah? Jeremiah openly wonders how much judgment it will take for the nation to repent. Have you ever wondered the same thing about someone you know? How did old Honest come to repentance?

2. Great Heart and Honest discuss the trials of a mutual companion, Mr. Fearing, a troubled pilgrim whose fear constantly hampered his journey. Yet his fear was not of worldly dangers like the lions, the Valley of Humiliation, or Vanity Fair. His fear revolved around doubts of his own salvation, or rather being accepted into the Celestial City. Read 1 John 5:11–13, Romans 10:13, Ephesians 1:13–14, and John 6:47. Write out below why you are confident in the assurance of your salvation.

3. Christiana, Mercy, and the boys are all glad to hear that Fearing arrived safely at the Celestial City despite his fears because they, too, battle similar fears. Great Heart said that proper fear is the beginning of wisdom (Proverbs 9:10). How does the fear of the Lord—reverential awe of Him—motivate us to choose wisdom over folly in our Christian walk?

Chapter 20: Mr. Self Will

1. Honest presents the tale of a wayward man, Mr. Self Will, whom he believes never entered at the Wicket Gate and only claimed to be a pilgrim. Self Will did whatever he pleased, believing that a pilgrim could live however they want, regardless of whether it was right or wrong, and no argument could persuade him otherwise. Have you ever had a friend or family member express the same presumptive attitude? How did you handle it? What sobering truth do we find from Jesus in Matthew 7:23?

2. Self Will backed up his claims of living how he wanted by twisting Scripture to justify his own sinful behavior. What biblical examples did he try to twist to his favor? Great Heart said that someone that held to such beliefs was not only deluded but probably did not have genuine faith either. In what ways do people today use Scripture to justify sin in their lives or in the lives of others?

3. Christiana mentioned the prevailing thought of some, that there's plenty of time to repent from your sins before you die. What are the usual concerns with sickbed repentance? Do you think a person who puts off repentance until their final hours of life can still receive salvation? Using Hosea 7:14, what does God compare this kind of repentance to?

Session 5: Approaching Vanity

In this week's readings, the pilgrims emerge from the valleys to stay in the home of an old disciple named Gaius for about a month. During this time, the men set out to find a menacing giant named Slay Good, who has been endangering pilgrims along the Way. They defeat the giant and rescue Mr. Feeble Mind, who joins their group. Before leaving the inn, Matthew and Mercy are married, and Gaius's daughter is married to James. Ready-to-halt also joins their group as a companion for Feeble Mind. When they reach the town of Vanity, the pilgrims stay with Mr. Mnason and meet other good people in the town. Their stay in Vanity differs from that of Christian's, in that the town celebrates them as heroes for defeating a beast who was killing men and kidnapping children. After many years, with the boys all fully grown and married, they leave Vanity, arriving at By-Path Meadow. There, the men successfully slay Giant Despair and his wife, Dissident, and free Mr. Despondency and his daughter, Much-afraid, from the giant's dungeon.

Session 5 Chapters

Chapter 21: Welcomed by Gaius
Chapter 22: Slay Good and Feeble Mind
Chapter 23: Good Samaritan's Promise
Chapter 24: The Church in Vanity
Chapter 25: Storming Doubting Castle

Chapter 21: Welcomed by Gaius

1. Honest leads the group of pilgrims to an inn owned by an old disciple named Gaius, who loves to shelter pilgrims and readily welcomes them. Read Romans 16:23 and 3 John. What similarities do you see between the Gaius in Scripture and the one from Bunyan's story? Do you enjoy opening up your home to other believers? What are some common excuses that keep us from doing so?

2. In Gaius's long defense of women, what are some of his arguments for why we shouldn't overlook the prominent role of women in both the Old and New Testaments? How might churches do a better job helping young women understand they are endowed and pursued with grace and special favor from God?

3. Gaius gives great honor to the legacy of Christian and of his great lineage of ancestors and tells the family of the noble line of martyrs from whom they descend. In these books, Bunyan uses "Christian" as a surname for the family of believers. The Christian lineage of faithful believers that Gaius mentions is also our lineage. In Galatians 3:26–29, Paul says all those who are in Christ are sons and daughters of God through faith. They are a family. How should your identity as a believer—your Christian lineage—impact your faith and your relationship with other believers?

Chapter 22: Slay Good and Feeble Mind

1. When Great Heart learns that a brutal, flesh-eating giant named Slay Good has been ravaging local pilgrims, he leads an expedition to kill the villain. Both here and again later with Giant Despair, we see the pilgrims intentionally exposing themselves to danger rather than responding to what they encounter along the Way. What does Paul say in Ephesians 5:11 about a Christian's responsibility to expose the darkness in our culture? How will culture automatically respond? Do you find it hard to speak out against the evil you see around you?

2. The pilgrims rescue Mr. Feeble Mind, who Slay Good is tormenting in a cave. Feeble Mind is a sickly man in mind and body but not in spirit. His weakness doesn't stop him from embarking on a pilgrimage to heaven, and he's determined to get there even if he must crawl. Paul instructs us in 2 Corinthians 5:7 to walk by faith, not by sight. Describe a time when, because of depression, sadness, grief, rejection, or deception, you felt all you could do was crawl to Jesus. What encouragement does Romans 8:26 offer when you're feeling ambushed by the reality that nothing is certain?

3. Feeble Mind's companion, Mr. Not Right, abandoned him when Slay Good attacked. However, later he was struck by lightning and killed. Slay Good inadvertently saved Feeble Mind's life by capturing him. The doctrine of divine providence asserts that an all-wise, all-loving God is in complete control of our lives and has a plan for us that fits into His ultimate purpose. Read Romans 8:28–29. What are some surprising things you've learned about yourself during times of crises or intense pressure? How has God used those difficulties and trials for your good?

Chapter 23: Good Samaritan's Promise

1. As they prepare to leave the inn, Gaius refuses any kind of payment for his hospitality, citing the Good Samaritan's promise. Read Luke 10:25–37. Jesus is the Good Samaritan who rescued us from the road of certain death and paid to restore us to health. He tells us to do likewise. Describe a time when you needed a good Samaritan like Gaius to provide you with rest to heal from the hardships of life. Who is someone you can be a good Samaritan to?

2. As they set out to leave Gaius's home, why did Feeble Mind tell Great Heart he wished to stay behind? Paul tells us in 1 Thessalonians 5:14 and Romans 14 that we have a strong obligation to bear with the failings of the weaker Christian. What activities can cause friction between Christians today? How do you balance the need to stand for your liberty as a Christian while avoiding hurting the walks of others?

3. Just as they are about to resume their journey, they meet a man named Ready-to-halt, a handicapped pilgrim who walks with the aid of crutches and who becomes a suitable companion for Feeble Mind. What is Feeble Mind's response when Ready-to-halt offers to let him use one of his crutches? What do you think the crutches represent?

Chapter 24: The Church in Vanity

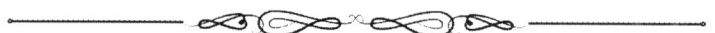

1. The growing band of pilgrims entered Vanity and stayed at the home of Mr. Mnason, who introduced them to other God-fearing residents of the town. The church in Vanity was small but soon had a considerable impact on the community. In Acts 17:6, we learn that the first century church had turned the world upside down for Christ. They didn't do it with protests, marches, or boycotts; they did it through the faithful proclamation of the gospel! According to Acts 2:3 and 4:32–35, what did those early Christians have that we need today? What does it look like to be on fire for God?

2. When a seven-headed beast emerges from the woods, killing townspeople and carrying off children, Great Heart and the men pursue and mortally wound the evil creature. The beast appears as expected during its usual seasons, but the brave men keep engaging it until eventually the wounded monster retreats. In some form or fashion, evil will continue to rear its ugly head. What manifestations of evil do you see in today's culture that are killing adults and luring children to themselves? How do you defeat these?

3. How was Christiana and her group's experience in Vanity different from that of Christian and Faithful? Christian's determination to stay strong in the faith and Faithful's martyrdom seemed to have paved the way for new pilgrims entering Vanity. What did the martyrdom of Stephen lead to in Acts 8:1–4 and the fulfillment of Jesus' command in Acts 1:8?

Chapter 25: Storming Doubting Castle

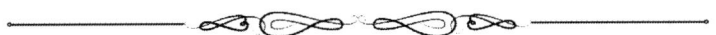

1. The pilgrims arrive at the field before the Delectable Mountains. There, Christiana instructs her daughters to commit their little ones to the care of the shepherd who dwells here. In Mark 10:13–16, we find parents bringing their children to Jesus. He holds them, prays for them, and tells his disciples to welcome them. Who has the primary responsibility for the spiritual development of children? What does it mean to commit your child to God? In what practical ways do you bring your children or grandchildren to Jesus?

2. When the pilgrims draw near to By-path Meadow, Great Heart and the men decide to put an end to the evil of Doubting Castle. After slaying Giant Despair and his wife, Dissidence, they take seven days to destroy the castle and free Mr. Despondency and his daughter, Much-afraid, from the dungeon. What do you think of the decision to attack Giant Despair? What does this tell us about confronting and fighting our own bouts with the enemies of despair and depression? What encouragement does Deuteronomy 20:3–4 offer us when fighting those enemies?

3. Upon the men's triumphant return, Christiana and Mercy serenade the heroic men on the viol and lute. Throughout the book, we find the pilgrims celebrating when evil is overcome then placing up markers of remembrance for future pilgrims. Why is it important to celebrate and mark our freedom from those things that have oppressed us?

Session 6: Nearing the End

In this week's readings, the pilgrims reach the Delectable Mountains, where they meet a group of shepherds who show them everything shown to Christian plus more wonders of the land. Now in their last stretch to the Celestial City, they encounter a pilgrim named Valiant-for-truth, who was badly beaten while fending off an attack in the same place where Little Faith had been robbed. Great Heart invites the brave warrior to join their group. As they get closer to the Enchanted Ground, they want to rest, but Great Heart wisely presses them forward, aided by his map that details the way to the Celestial City. As they reach the end of the Enchanted Ground, they encounter a man named Standfast, who, through prayer, had just overcome the temptations of Madam Bubble. Arriving in the Land of Beulah, their now large group comes to the River of Death, where each pilgrim takes their turn crossing over, except for Christiana's boys and their wives, who stay behind to support the church.

Session 6 Chapters

Chapter 26: The View from the Mountains
Chapter 27: Valiant's Zeal for Truth
Chapter 28: The Enchanted Ground
Chapter 29: The Land of Beulah
Chapter 30: The Pilgrims Receive a Summons

Chapter 26: The View from the Mountains

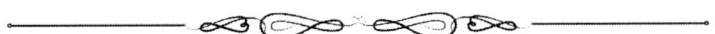

1. For both Christian and Christiana, the Delectable Mountains represent a maturing of their faith when their vantage point is wider and they can see the world differently than before. In 2 Kings 6:17, Elisha prays for God to open his servant's eyes. What can the servant see around him that he could not before? Like the servant, fear and panic can easily consume us when viewing life with our physical eyes. What life situations do you view differently as you have matured as a Christian? Where does God still need to open your eyes?

2. The Shepherds show the pilgrims the wonders of the land—those shown to Christian and new ones as well. Describe what the pilgrims see and learn at each mountain below and, using the Scripture verse, what each allegory teaches the pilgrims.

Mount Marvel (Mark 11:23–24)

Mount Innocent (Matthew 5:11–12)

Mount Charity (1 Kings 17:13–16)

3. Mercy is pregnant and finds herself fascinated and longing for a mirror she finds at the Shepherds' palace and believes she will miscarry if she doesn't have it. Normally an irrational desire for a mirror could be interpreted as vanity, yet this scene portrays it as commendable. What is special about this mirror? James describes the Word as a mirror in James 1:23–25. What is the mirror of Scripture supposed to reflect? What is the problem with using the mirror of the Word passively?

Chapter 27: Valiant's Zeal for Truth

1. The pilgrims meet a bruised and bloody man named Valiant-for-truth after he has defeated three men trying to keep him from reaching the Celestial City. The man fought well because he had an excellent weapon that could penetrate flesh, bone, soul, and spirit. How do Hebrews 4:12 and Ephesians 6:17 describe God's Word? Why might dividing the soul and spirit be an important function of God's Word? What does Valiant's long, bloody battle teach us about spiritual warfare?

2. We learn that Christian's own pilgrimage inspired Valiant to leave his hometown of Darkland and take his own journey of faith. Great Heart commends him for tuning out those who would dissuade him from his journey, including his own parents who tried to stop him, telling of all the dangers that awaited him. If you had a child who believed God was calling them into missions, specifically to a dangerous area, how would you counsel them?

3. Most of the warnings presented by Valiant's parents were true except for Christian drowning in the river. Christ clearly made known the risks of following him multiple times, including John 16:2, John 15:19, and many others. The risk that Christian took on his own pilgrimage helped Valiant come to faith. Think about your own life. Who took a risk on you and helped you come to know Jesus? What can you learn from his or her example?

Chapter 28: The Enchanted Ground

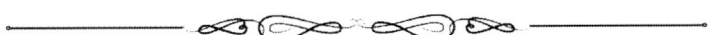

1. The pilgrims enter the Enchanted Ground with their swords drawn and on high alert. Describe some dangers of the Enchanted Ground. Why does it seem to be associated more with pilgrims toward the end of their journey? How might the spiritual complacency of the older generation become harmful and even dangerous to the church?

2. As the group emerges from the Enchanted Ground, they encounter a man named Standfast, who, through prayer, is standing his ground against the allurements of a dangerous temptress. In the first century, the smallest Roman military battle unit comprised sixteen men spaced six feet apart. They trained each soldier to stand their ground and not let an enemy soldier enter their six feet of space. As long as they stood together and didn't break ranks, their legions were considered virtually invincible. How might this have influenced Paul's writings to "stand our ground" in Ephesians 6:11–13? How could standing in truth have helped you in a recent conflict or challenge?

3. Standfast tells the pilgrims of his run-in with Madam Bubble, the enchantress who oversees the Enchanted Grounds. She's the last enemy encountered on the Way and is wealthy, well-spoken, attractive, greedy, and promiscuous. She offers Standfast her body, her money, and the promise of happiness. Bunyan clearly modeled her description after the adulteress in Proverbs 5–7, representing the seduction the world has toward Christians. In James 4:4, James refers to people pursuing a worldly lifestyle as adulterous. How do we avoid being friends with the world while still being in the world? Does this mean that we shouldn't be friends with unbelievers or embrace modern technology and medical advances or wear certain clothing?

Chapter 29: The Land of Beulah

1. The Land of Beulah is the closest a pilgrim can get to the Celestial City in this earthly life and is where they wait to be summoned to advance to the Celestial Gate. Even though the land appeals to all the senses and is full of light, wonderful smells, delicacies, music, and singing, its purpose is to prepare pilgrims to cross the River of Death. When they cross the river, the water tastes bitter at first than sweet when swallowed. How is death for the Christian both bitter and sweet? In 1 Thessalonians 4:13, what proper balance does Paul say a Christian should maintain when discussing death? Do you struggle to contemplate your own death? Explain.

2. Christiana is the first to be summoned by the King to cross the river. Before she goes, she prepares herself for her journey by first blessing her children and speaking to each pilgrim individually, even telling some of them difficult things. Nearing his death, Jacob gathered his family together and pronounced blessings on his sons but also relived positive and negative moments (Genesis 49:1–28). Have you ever thought about what kind of blessings your children or grandchildren need to receive from you before your death? Would there be any difficult conversations to have with some?

3. In current Western culture, life expectancy for men is around 75 years of age, whereas in Bunyan's time, it was 50–55 years of age. As we live longer, death becomes more mysterious and feared, but for those in Bunyan's era, death was a common occurrence happening even to the young. Most people had spent time with someone that was dying. Share an experience of being with someone close to death. What feelings did they share with you? Were they confident in their faith, or did they seem more distressed? How did their death affect you in the moment?

Chapter 30: The Pilgrims Receive a Summons

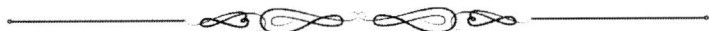

1. As each pilgrim is summoned to cross the river, they are given a sign from Ecclesiastes 12:2–7, which most agree is a poetic description of the effects of advancing age. Describe what you think each verse is referring to regarding the aging process.

Ready-to-halt – Severed Silver Cord (Ecc. 12:6)

Feeble Mind – Windows Growing Dim (Ecc. 12:3)

Despondency – Grasshopper (Ecc. 12:5)

Honest – Songs Growing Faint (Ecc. 12:4)

Valiant – Broken Pitcher (Eccles. 12:6)

2. In some cultures, a person's last words are often written down and preserved. Examine the last words of each of the pilgrims. What would you want your last words to be? Which of the characters in this story do you most identify with and why?

3. Christiana's sons and their wives stay behind to grow the church on Earth. Because of Christian's faith, his family went in one generation from being an unbelieving family to being a family with a Christian heritage. What hope does this offer you for lost or broken homes today? How has God used this study to teach you more about yourself and your own journey of faith?

Leave a Review

Thank you again for doing this Bible study! I hope and pray that in some way, it encouraged you (and your group) to grow closer to Christ.

If you enjoyed this study, I would appreciate your leaving an honest review for the book and study on Amazon! Your review will help others know if this study is right for them and their small group.

It's easy and will only take a minute. Just search for "The Pilgrim's Progress Part 2 Study Guide, Alan Vermilye" on Amazon. Click on the product in the search results, and then click on reviews.

I would also love to hear from you! Drop me a note by visiting me at www.BrownChairBooks.com and clicking on "Contact."

Thank you and God bless!

Alan

Get the Entire Pilgrim's Progress Series

Click on any of the Bible studies below to learn more or to download sample chapters visit us at
www.BrownChairBooks.com

Book Series

Study Guide Series

Audio Series

Other Studies from Brown Chair Books

On the following pages, you'll find information from some of our other Bible studies.

www.BrownChairBooks.com

THE PILGRIM'S PROGRESS
A Readable Modern–Day Version of John Bunyan's Pilgrim's Progress
By Alan Vermilye

Reading *The Pilgrim's Progress* by John Bunyan can be a bit challenging even for the best of readers. Not so with this new, easy–to–read version that translates the original archaic language into simple conversational English allowing readers of all ages to easily navigate the most popular Christian allegory of all time.

Without losing any faithfulness to the original text, now you can read Bunyan's timeless classic and reimagine this famous quest that has challenged and encouraged believers for centuries.

Audio Book also available!

What others are saying:

Phenomenal! Finally, able to read The Pilgrims Progress!!! – Sandra

What a blessing! Definitely one of the ten books that I have ever read. – TC

Wow!! This book lights a fire in your heart for sure. Thank you, Alan for an accurate revision so that I may understand. – Jesse

Try reading this book, if you dare. You will find you identify with more than one characters in the book. – Jon

www.BrownChairBooks.com

THE PILGRIM'S PROGRESS STUDY GUIDE
A Bible Study Based on John Bunyan's Pilgrim's Progress
By Alan Vermilye

Understanding *The Pilgrim's Progress* by John Bunyan can be difficult and confusing at times. Not so with *The Pilgrim's Progress Study Guide*! This comprehensive Bible study workbook will guide you through Bunyan's masterful use of metaphors helping you better understand key concepts, supporting Bible passages, and the relevance to our world today.

Designed to be used alongside *The Pilgrim's Progress: A Readable Modern–Day Version of John Bunyan's Pilgrim's Progress*, each chapter, sub section, and study question examines Bunyan's allegorical narrative to tell his powerful presentation of what it means to follow the narrow way of Christian salvation.

What others are saying:

This was a tour de force trip through scripture with rich discussions each week. I highly recommend it! – Stan

Invaluable book! My wife and I started rereading The Pilgrims Progress, so I got this study guide, so happy I did! Great study questions you make you think. — Mark

I heartily recommend the combination of Pilgrim's Progress and Pilgrim's Progress Study Guide by Alan Vermilye. You'll be glad you took the time to do this study. – Paul

www.BrownChairBooks.com

THE PRACTICE OF THE PRESENCE OF GOD
A 40–Day Devotion Based on Brother Lawrence's The Practice of the Presence of God
By Alan Vermilye

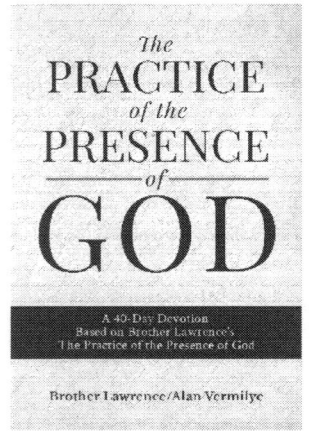

Since it was first published in 1691, *The Practice of the Presence of God* contains a collection of notes, letters, and interviews given by Brother Lawrence to his friends as a way of helping them turn ordinary daily life events into conversations with God.

Based on this timeless classic, *The Practice of the Presence of God: A 40–Day Devotion* guides readers on a 40–day journey through the wisdom of Brother Lawrence, related Scripture passages, and devotional thoughts that bring you into a more conversational relationship with God.

What others are saying:

I love this devotional. It is short and to the point, and thus making it easy to stick to every day! – Kathleen

Enlightening new depths in prayer. – Kathy

This devotional opens the door to Brother Lawrence that brings his letters and conversations to life every day! – Steve

www.BrownChairBooks.com

MERE CHRISTIANITY STUDY GUIDE
A Bible Study on the C.S. Lewis Book *Mere Christianity*
By Steven Urban

Mere Christianity Study Guide takes participants through a study of C.S. Lewis's classic, *Mere Christianity*. Despite its recognition as a "classic," there is surprisingly little available today in terms of a serious study course.

This 12–week Bible study digs deep into each chapter and, in turn, into Lewis's thoughts. Perfect for small group sessions, this interactive workbook includes daily, individual study as well as a complete appendix and commentary to supplement and further clarify certain topics. Multiple–week format options are also included.

What others are saying:

This study guide is more than just a guide to C.S Lewis's Mere Christianity*; it is a guide to Christianity itself.* – Crystal

Wow! What a lot of insight and food for thought! Perfect supplement to Mere Christianity. *I think Mr. Lewis himself would approve.* – Laurie

Our group is in the middle of studying Mere Christianity, *and I have found this guide to be invaluable.* – Angela

This is a very useful and comprehensive guide to Mere Christianity. – John

www.BrownChairBooks.com

THE SCREWTAPE LETTERS STUDY GUIDE
A Bible Study on the C.S. Lewis Book *The Screwtape Letters*
By Alan Vermilye

The Screwtape Letters Study Guide takes participants through a study of C.S. Lewis's classic, *The Screwtape Letters*.

This Bible study digs deep into each letter from Screwtape, an undersecretary in the lowerarchy of hell, to his incompetent nephew, Wormwood, a junior devil. Perfect for small group sessions, this interactive workbook includes daily, individual study with a complete answer guide available online.

Designed as a 12–week study, multiple–week format options are also included.

What others are saying:

This book and study create a positive reinforcement on fighting that spiritual battle in life. Great read, great study guide! – Lester

This study guide was a wonderful way for our group to work through The Screwtape Letters*!* – Becky

Use this Study Guide for a fresh "seeing" of The Screwtape Letters*!* – William

This is an essential companion if you are reading The Screwtape Letters *as a small group.* – J.T.

www.BrownChairBooks.com

THE GREAT DIVORCE STUDY GUIDE
A Bible Study on the C.S. Lewis Book *The Great Divorce*
By Alan Vermilye

The Great Divorce Study Guide is an eight–week Bible study on the C.S. Lewis classic, *The Great Divorce*. Perfect for small groups or individual study, each weekly study session applies a biblical framework to the concepts found in each chapter of the book. Although intriguing and entertaining, much of Lewis's writings can be difficult to grasp.

The Great Divorce Study Guide will guide you through each one of Lewis's masterful metaphors to a better understanding of the key concepts of the book, the supporting Bible passages, and the relevance to our world today. Each study question is ideal for group discussion, and answers to each question are available online.

What others are saying:

To my knowledge, there have not been many study guides for either of these, so to see this new one on The Great Divorce *(both electronic and print) is a welcome sight!* – Richard

I recommend The Great Divorce Study Guide *to anyone or any group wishing to delve more deeply into the question, why would anyone choose hell over heaven!* – Ruth

The questions were thought–provoking, and I very much liked how everything was evaluated by scripture. Would definitely recommend! – Justin

www.BrownChairBooks.com

THE PROBLEM OF PAIN STUDY GUIDE

A Bible Study on the C.S. Lewis Book *The Problem of Pain*

By Alan Vermilye

Why must humanity suffer? Why doesn't God alleviate our pain, even some?

In his book, *The Problem of Pain*, C.S. Lewis's philosophical approach to why we experience pain can be confusing at times. *The Problem of Pain Study Guide* breaks down each chapter into easy–to–understand questions and commentary to help you find meaning and hope amid the pain.

The Problem of Pain Study Guide expands upon Lewis's elegant and thoughtful work, where he seeks to understand how a loving, good, and powerful God can possibly coexist with the pain and suffering that is so pervasive in the world and in our lives. As Christ–followers, we might expect the world to be just, fair, and less painful, but it is not. This is the problem of pain.

What others are saying:

Many thanks for lending me a helping hand with one of the greatest thinkers of all time! – Adrienne

The questions posed range from very straightforward (to help the reader grasp main concepts) to more probing (to facilitate personal application), while perhaps the greatest benefit they supply is their tie–in of coordinating scriptures that may not always be apparent to the reader. – Sphinn

The questions are thought–provoking and biblically based! – Jen

www.BrownChairBooks.com

A CHRISTMAS CAROL STUDY GUIDE
Book and Bible Study Based on *A Christmas Carol*
By Alan Vermilye

A Christmas Carol Book and Bible Study Guide includes the entire book of this Dickens classic as well as Bible study discussion questions for each chapter, Scripture references, and related commentary.

Detailed character sketches and an easy–to–read book summary provide deep insights into each character while examining the book's themes of greed, isolation, guilt, blame, compassion, generosity, transformation, forgiveness, and, finally, redemption. To help with those more difficult discussion questions, a complete answer guide is available for free online.

What others are saying:

The study is perfect for this time of the year, turning our focus to the reason for the season–Jesus–and the gift of redemption we have through him. – Connie

I used this for an adult Sunday School class. We all loved it! – John

This study is wonderful! – Lori

I found this a refreshing look at the Bible through the eyes of Ebenezer Scrooge's life. – Lynelle

www.BrownChairBooks.com

IT'S A WONDERFUL STUDY GUIDE
A Bible Study Based on the Christmas Classic *It's a Wonderful Life*
By Alan Vermilye

It's a Wonderful Life is one of the most popular and heartwarming films ever made. It's near universal appeal and association with Christmas has provided a rich story of redemption that has inspired generations for decades.

It's a Wonderful Life Study Guide examines this beloved holiday classic and reminds us how easily we can become distracted from what is truly meaningful in life. This five–week Bible study experience comes complete with discussion questions for each session, Scripture references, detailed character sketches, a movie summary, and related commentary. In addition, a complete answer guide and video segments for each session are available for free online.

What others are saying:

Thank you, Alan for, the unforgettable experience. Your book has prompted me to see and learn much more than merely enjoying the film, It's a Wonderful Life. *– Er Jwee*

The questions got us all thinking, and the answers provided were insightful and encouraging. I would definitely encourage Home Groups to study this! – Jill

It's a Wonderful Life Study Guide *by Alan Vermilye is intelligent, innovative, interesting, involving, insightful, and inspirational. – Paul*

www.BrownChairBooks.com

THE CAROLS OF CHRISTMAS

Daily Advent Devotions on Classic Christmas Carols
By Alan Vermilye

The Carols of Christmas is a heart-warming devotional inspired by some of the most beloved Christmas carols of all time. Inside, you'll enjoy a fresh glimpse of some of the same joyful and nostalgic melodies you sing every year now set to personal reflections in this 28-day devotional journey.

The book is divided into four weeks of daily devotions, perfect for celebrating Advent or Christmas. Each week you begin by reading the history of the carol, followed by six daily devotions that reflect on a verse from the hymn along with a Scripture reflection.

Traditionally, Advent begins on the fourth Sunday before Christmas, but the devotions are undated, allowing you to start at any time.

What others are saying:

"Well written, joyful, to the point, informative and inspiring. An annual read for Advent from now on. I loved all of it!!!" – Avid Reader

"This was perfect to read and end on Christmas Day! Everyone should read this one." – Janice

"My wife and I read through this Advent devotional this year and found it both interesting and inspiring. Grab one for next year!" – Randy

www.BrownChairBooks.com

Printed in Great Britain
by Amazon